D1234323

In Towns
and
Little Towns

In Towns and Little Towns

A Book of Poems
by
Father Leonard Feeney

Loreto Publications
Fitzwilliam, New Hampshire
A.D. 2004

Typesetting, Layout, and Design
Copyrighted and
Published by:
Loreto Publications
P. O. Box 603
Fitzwilliam, NH 03447
Phone: 603-239-6671
Fax: 603-239-6127
www.LoretoPubs.org

ISBN: 1-930278-42-X

Library of Congress Control Number: 2004108326

Printed and bound in the U.S.A.

Dedication

To my mother from her minstrel boy

Acknowledgements

For permission to reprint certain poems in this book, the author is grateful to the editors of the following periodicals:

America, Commonwealth, Harper's, Messenger of the Sacred Heart, Queen's Work, and *Thought.*

Table of Contents

Table of Contents

Table of Contents

In Towns and Little Towns

If there be pale princesses,
And ragged royalty;
And monarchs without money,
And pompless pedigree;

And queens without courtiers,
And kings without crowns,
Lord, make me laureate
In towns and little towns.

The Teacher

I drudge and toil — but I have my hour
    As I sit in my high backed chair,
With the wide, adoring eyes of youth
    Upon me there.

I tell them the tale of the mighty horse
    That straddled the gates of Troy,
And it puts the wonder on Timothy,
    The grocer's boy.

I tell them of fair Endymion
    Who slept by the mountain stream;
And little Hubert, the tinsmith's lad,
    Begins to dream.

And the tale of the winds and the Aulian maid
    Who died on the golden sands
Makes David, the baker's son, look up
    And wring his hands.

Oh, there is a dream that is lightly passed
    And one that will vanish not!
But what will become of the dreaming lads
    That I begot?

Who'll mend the kettles and pots and pans
    Forever and ever more?
And what will become of the baker's shop
    And the grocery store?

A Saint For Monday Morning

There's a little wooden clothes-rack
    That stands in our back hall,
Where a little wrinkled lady
    Hangs her bonnet and her shawl.
Every Monday very early,
    And she tip-toes unawares
To the laundry room, in silence,
    Down behind the kitchen stairs
      To scrub, scrub, scrub,
      In her little round tub.

Although the water spoils her dress
    And moistens her white hair,
Yet the laundry gets a fairy touch
    Somehow, when she is there.
For this little wrinkled lady
    Is so very small to see,
And both her shrunken hands are white
    As any bride's could be.
And her cheeks grow red as apples
    When the steam begins to rise
And the iridescent suds shine clear
    Reflected in her eyes;

A Saint for Monday Morning

With a hundred twinkling bubbles
  In the Monday morning sun
And a multicolored rainbow
  On the rim of every one.

And the pretty things she handles:
  Muslins, linens, lace and things;
And on her fingers soap crystals
  Make little diamond rings.
And when the steam begins to sing,
  She starts a-humming, too;
And they make a curious harmony,
  The steam and humming do,
    With the scrub, scrub, scrub,
    Of her little round tub.

And when she pours the blueing in
  And starts again to scrub,
You'd think it was a tiny sea,
  This little wooden tub.
And when the sparkling, soapy waves
  Keep splashing o'er and o'er,

A Saint for Monday Morning

You might fancy her a little girl
    Playing on the shore.
Ah, but little seashore maidens
    Do not have such snowy hair,
And none of them have foreheads dimmed
    Nor shoulders drooped with care,
Nor wrinkles that the long slow years
    Have grooved in painfully;
For a hard and weary life it is
    To be a wash-lady.

But there'll come a Monday morning
    When the little tub will rest,
And they'll fold two very tired hands
    Upon a tired breast.
And the angels will be telling her
    In God's eternity,
How He loved the music that she made,
    The dull monotony
        Of the scrub, scrub scrub,
        In her little round tub.

Achievement

Solon, Plato, Socrates—
    Where does your vaunted learning stand?
My grandfather was a schoolmaster
    In Ireland!

Tall legions, Roman Caesar's men—
    And trooped ye fearless to the sea?
My father's uncle brained a bull
    With the limb of an apple tree!

Fair handiwork of Raphael,
    Delicate still while ages pass—
My grandmother knitted the silken stole
    A priest wore once for holy Mass.

Temples and shrines of the dreamy East:
    A tower will fall if man begin it;
The thatched cottage of my sires
    Had two real windows in it!

And Orpheus, thou poor lutanist,
    For all thy windy lyre played,—
My father whistled a little tune
    And he won a better maid!

Love's Young Dream

Did you recall, Methuselah
    When you were white and old
A maid, a moonlit night and a
    Sweet vow you told?

Methuselah, did you recall
    The song your heart had sung,
When she was fair, and love was all,
    And you were young?

And count each lonely century,
    And live the days again
When you were a hundred and twenty, and she
    A hundred and ten!

To a Blacksmith

Had I the brawn, not linened and laundered
    In fashion, these idle times,
Would I bide the hour—my strength all squandered
    On rhymes.
With the loan of your hammer to smite with a dreadful
    Swing on the molten bars,
I would people the dingy air with a shedful
    Of stars!

A Forgotten Birthday
(For Eileen)

Oh, the seventeenth of August,
　　How could I forget, my dear!
Not an angel up in Heaven
　　But remembered it I fear.

Not a single white-winged angel
　　But was very much aware
Of your birthday—by the music,
　　By the fragrance in the air.

Yet the seventeenth of August,
　　It completely passed me by:
I never even noticed it
　　Nor stopped to wonder why.

And yet I had a reason
　　For forgetting don't you see,
For the seventeenth of August
　　Has been pretty mean to me.

For it prowls around each summer
　　With its sly, secretive smile,
And bit by bit it's plundering
　　A little girl, the while.

A Forgotten Birthday

And bit by bit it's trying hard
    To make her old and wise
And shut the world of fairyland
    Forever from her eyes.

I am going to take the calendar
    That hangs upon the wall
And cut the seventeenth of August
    Out —for once and all.

Oh! The seventeenth of August!
    I despise and hate it so;
I wish I had forgotten it
    A dozen years ago.

And maybe you would still be seven
    Or maybe you'd be eight,
And every night I'd come and find you
    Swinging on the gate.

Night Noises

Angela died today and went to Heaven;
  We counted her summers up and they were seven.
But why does that trouble you, unloosened shutter,
  That flap at my window in the wind's wild flutter!

Angela's eyes tonight are cold and dim,
  Off in the land of song and Seraphim.
But what does that mean to you, O creaking stair,
  And mice in the wall that gnaw the plaster there!

Angela's little hands are folded white,
  Deep in the meadow, under the starry night.
But why should an ugly gnat keep finely whining
  Around the candle-flame beside me shining!

And never again — and never again will she
  Come running across the field to welcome me.
But, little sheep-bells, out on the distant hill,
  Why, at this hour, do you wake and tinkle still!

And not any more—alas!— and not any more,
  Will she climb the stairs and knock at my lonely door.
But, moaning owl in the hayloft overhead,
  How did you come to know that she was dead!

Vanity

She sat one morn by a looking-glass
    Watching her youth and her beauty pass;
And she spied on her cheek a pallor repose
    And she powdered it o'er with a radiant rose.

She sat one noon by a mirror pool
    Watching the light in her eyes grow cool;
And she spied on her forehead a silver hair
    And she tucked it away in complete despair.

She sat one eve by a starlit well
    Watching the charm that the years dispel;
And she spied a wee wrinkle run over her face
    And she rubbed it out quickly in utter disgrace.

She slept one night in a narrow grave
    Watching the poppies and lilies wave;
And a dandelion over her head she spied
    And she smothered its roots till it withered and died!

Lunacy

Sweeter than moons or accurate planets swing
    In rhythmic, pale, parabolas of light,
I count a lone star in its wandering
    Along the trackless orbit of the night.
And sometimes wise men chattering away
    Things true, coherent and proper — I hold less
Than a poor little mind bewildered and astray
    From love or grief or utter loneliness.

The Geranium

If you wish to grow a lily
    With its white and golden hue
You will have to have a mansion
    And a gardener or two.

If you fondle a chrysanthemum
    From Spring to early Fall,
It may consent to bloom a bit,
    If it ever blooms at all.

A rose must have a radiant bush
    With lots of room and air;
And a peony wants the terrace
    Of a multimillionaire;

But all a poor geranium
    Will ever ask a man—
Is a little bit of fragrant earth
    And an old tomato can.

Recipe for a Butterfly

Cut two radiant strips of rainbow veil
  From heaven high;
Dip them first in a rose's, then in a violet's blood,
  The while they lie;
Scatter them o'er with the powder caught from a
    moony mist
  And let them dry.
Reach up above and pull two little, gold starry eyes
  Out of the sky.
The whole throw gently into the breath of a garden
    wind,—
  And it will fly!!

The Altar Boy

His cheeks grow red from the candle heat
As the carpet under his noiseless feet.

And no two stars could be half so bright
As his deep brown eyes in the candle-light.

An angel he seems with his surplice wings,
Who knows when God is to come,—and rings.

And the clouds from the censer swinging there
A fragrance leave in his golden hair.

It fills us all with a wondrous dread,
His nearness unto the Holy Bread.

Now I wonder what path in life he'll plan:
A doctor—a lawyer—a merchantman?

God keep him always there we pray,
Treading the altar's plush highway.

Wealth

You can buy a rubber ball
　　　For a penny.
Oh the wonder of it all
　　　For a penny!
Or a whistle or a gun
Or a sugar-coated bun—
You can have a lot of fun
　　　For a penny.

You can wear a jewelled pin
　　　For a penny;
And you're fifty dollars in
　　　For a penny.
You can find how much you weigh,
Read the gossip of the day,
And a music-box will play
　　　For a penny.

Wealth

You can drive away the night
    For a penny,
With a stick of candlelight
    For a penny.
When the circus comes in June
You can buy a toy balloon;
Send it floating to the moon—
    For a penny.

All the pleasure, who can guess
    For a penny!
Who can count the happiness
    For a penny!
Why this striving after gold?
Life is yours to have and hold;
You can have your fortune told—
    For a penny!

Prayer of a Crossing Tender

God help a poor old man to guard
　　The traffic of the town.
May God give strength to my right arm
　　To swing the white gates down.

God make my eyes alert to see
　　From break o' dawn till night,
And watch the steps of little tots
　　Who are my heart's delight.

But oh, when Mistress Guzzlegold
　　Comes knocking at my shack
Enquiring if her fluffy dog
　　May safely cross the track:

May God forgive the likes of me
　　For ever taking pains
In trying to keep the likes of her
　　From being hit by trains.

The Traffic Cop
(From a Servant-Girl)

He said to me, "Fair Maiden,
    And what is it you do?"
I said, "I'm a living-out girl
    On Fifth Avenue."

He said, "I've rarely seen a maid
    With so much sweetness in her."
I said, "I'd like to cross the road
    And hurry home for dinner!"

He looked at me and raised his hand:
    Ah, Lord, and who am I
That millionaires in motor-cars
    Should stop to let me by?

One gesture from his noble hand,
    One swift look at the throng
And the roadway clears like magic
    And the people move along.

I dreamt of him, and in my dreams
    He stood in worlds afar;
He kept the planets in their course
    And star from striking star!

And little hoped a timid maid
    As plain as I to win him;
He's so beautiful and mighty—
    There is some archangel in him.

The Traffic Cop

But one night when Fifth Avenue
     And all its roar was still,
I heard his shiny whistle blow
     Beneath my window-sill.

I ran from the lonely kitchen
     And let the curtain drop—
And put my hand into the hand
     That makes the whole world STOP.

A song of love he sang to me;
     His words were sweet and low;
I did not dare resist the voice
     That makes the whole world GO.

I ran away to be his bride,
     My heart was all a-quiver—
Now I'm climbing seven flights of stairs
     Beside the Harlem River.

If you see a big policeman,
     You people passing by,
With a wistful look upon him—
     You will know the reason why.

He is tired of the cross-streets
     And lonely in the noise;
And he's longing for the traffic
     Of his little girls and boys.

The Family Overhead

They blew on bugles, beat on drums,
    And slammed each separate door.
They walked a hundred elephants
    Across the kitchen floor.

They talked the talk of Babylon
    And fought the fights of Troy;
They slaughtered sleep, they clubbed repose
    And murdered peace and joy.

They nearly made me lunatic,
    And well I blessed the day
Three burly moving-men drove up
    And carted them away. . . .

The family overhead is gone
    But I sit and wonder still
About the little yellow bird
    That used to cheep and trill.

And I wonder about the lullaby
    A woman used to sing,
That sounded, quiet afternoons,
    As sweet as anything.

And I wonder about the tiny feet
    That pattered on the stairs;
And the lilt and drawl at candle-time
    Of somebody's "good-night prayers."

And I wonder why is it the din of life
    Will so engross a man,
He'll let its music and melody
    Slip off in a moving-van.

A Pair of Spectacles

Her eyes are strained from sewing and from mending,
    My mother sees a mist upon the sea.
My mother sees a haze upon the meadow,
    And a filmy web on each uncertain tree.

Her eyes are tired from watching and from weeping,
    My mother sees a cloud across the sun;
And very dimly she beholds the starlight
    At evening, when the dreary day is done.

And last night as I stood there in her doorway,—
    I flickered, and my shroud she seemed to see.
And now she wears her little gold-rimmed spectacles
    Whenever she looks at me!

The Deathbed

Lord, was there need of a bitter thorn
    To pierce her heart,
She who is withered and weak and worn
    And broken apart!

Why is the night so dark and no sky
    To brighten her,
  When You know that it takes but a little cry
    To frighten her!

  When the smallest straw would have bent her low
    So frail and cold,
Why must You now a mountain throw
    On one so old!

See how the rivulet wrinkles run,
    And will You place
Another and yet another one
    On her tired face!

Hush! cried the woman, the hour of three
    Is nigh for me!
He is up on the arms of a splintered tree
    In the sky for me!
I am helping His mother to stand till He
    Will die for me!

The Rivals

And now Veronica Johnson
    Has gone to be a nun,
After all the time I've spent on her
    And all the things I've done.

I courted Veronica Johnson
    And gave her books and flowers,
And I loaned her my new umbrella
    To take her home in showers.

I trimmed the rose-bush at her door;
    I often mowed the grass.
And she had me wearing medals
    And trotting off to Mass.

But when I asked her for her hand
    She never gave a nod;
She threw me down completely
    And went running off with God.

Would you think that one so cruel
    Could ever, ever be—
With her highfalutin notions
    About eternity!

She said it was her Maker
    Who bade her leave and go.
Good Lord, unless you make a girl
    You haven't got a show.

The Ashcart

In search of beauty, truth and art,
　　For which I hold my pen in trust,
I wonder would I dare to sing
　　About a wagon-load of dust!

About a human fireside,
　　Its love and laughter sifted down
And smothered up in chimney smoke,
　　And slowly carted out of town!

I wonder is this rumbling pile,
　　This ugly little charnel heap,
Too lowly for the charm of verse—
　　Too unromantically cheap!

And should a poet tell a man
　　Who drives an ashcart in the square
He may not dream of fairyland,
　　Of what is beautiful and fair?

And must the wonder of his soul
　　Be stifled in this withered pyre,
Because his body is not clean,
　　Because his clothes are burnt with fire?

Then would a poet rob a man
　　Of every hope and high surprise,
And brush the sunshine from his face
　　And throw more ashes in his eyes.

Since when are we immaculate,
　　Who make a verse and turn a rhyme,

The Ashcart

That we should hurl our scorn at him
    Who wheels away the Summertime;

Who chariots autumn leaves to rest,
    The flowers of June, the buds of May;
Who fumbles in the ruined wreck
    Of trinkets we have thrown away;

Old China cups and parasols,
    And tattered books that once were new;—
A faded gown, and old man's hat,
    A little baby's broken shoe;—

A picture of your mother's youth;
    The way she used to hold her head;
The crumpled wreaths that heroes wore,
    The charred love-letters of the dead!

The whistle of the lark is heard
    Across the Monday morning sky:—
His children hold the ashman's hand,
    A woman kisses him good-bye.

And with their image in his heart
    He takes his last look at the light
And leaps upon his wagon seat
    And drives into his smoky night.

He fights for bread, he fights for breath,
    His hands are wrinkled up with pain.
He fights the meanest foes of life:
    Ingratitude and man's disdain.

He feeds upon the furnace blast,
    The tear-drops on his eyelids burn.

The Undertaker

He hears the trumpet call of time:
"And unto dust thou shalt return."

Lift up your head — poor, lowly man!
You and your little wagon lend
A spell of wonderment to life,
And every poet is your friend.

Look up across the clean, blue sky!
Then shall your glory be unfurled:—
When snow-white angels carry off
The broken ashes of the world!

The Undertaker

Scrawny and thin my dead come in
But looks are soon forgotten:
I fill the hollows in their cheeks
With little bits of cotton.

I set their hair a-waving fair
And draw their eyelids down,
And like a sculptor ply my art
Removing scowl and frown.

For death is brief and so is grief;
The tomb is no disgrace:
And every man I bury wears
A smile upon his face.

The Fireman

A gaudy helmet, burnished bright,
    Is plumed upon his head;
A jacket blue with buttons gold,
    A shirt of fiery red.
Now is the commonest of men
    Grotesquely garmented.

Grant him, ye poets, graciously
    Your tribute and acclaim,
Who, finding similarity
    Of trades, puts on the same
Wild vesture as the radiant moth
    That rushes to the flame.

The Baker's Window

Stars in many sizes—
    Half a moon on high:
Little tarts and muffins
    And a broken pie.

Double rings for Saturn
    Wheeling by the sun:
Two tremendous doughnuts
    And a frosted bun.

Silver streaks of star dust
    In a planet's wake:
Scatterings of sugar
    From a birthday cake.

Count how many sweet rolls
    In the sky you see;
Golden crumbs upon a cloth
    Spread for you and me.

Clear the shelf when morning
    Puts the stars to rout.
Now the Baker's window
    Is all sold out!

The Teller's Wife

I've a little squirrel keeps
    Me company.
I've a little yellow bird
    To sing for me.

Counting money in the bank
    My man's engaged.
Everything I love in life
    Is caged.

The Beggar's Ultimatum

If more pennies don't drop
    In my little tin cup,
I'll tell all the blind men
    In town to pack up.

And off we'll go leaving
    The whole crowd of you;
And you won't have any blind men,
    And then what'll you do?

A Document
(For My Mother)

Here's something may be told
    When you are old:
    Someone who loves you took
    A little book,
    Once upon a time,
    And wrote a rhyme
    About the winsome way,
    In moonlight, in May,
    You used to wear
    A white rose in your hair.

If anyone should doubt
    The loveliness I sing about,
    When youth has flown
    And left you by the fire alone;
    If no one can recall
    The May, the moonlight, or the rose at all—
    Let this poor rhyme be lent
    For document,
    When your step is slow,
    And your hair is snow.

Twelve O'Clock

At midnight in the hospital
    A little nun in white
Came tip-toe down the corridor
    Bearing a candle-light.

At twelve o'clock with noiseless step
    She passed from bed to bed,
And held a light at each man's face
    For fear he might be dead.

And some men sighed and some men moaned,
    And some began to pray,
To show the little nun in white
    They had not passed away.

But there were some who made no moan
    Although they did survive;
And there was one who thought he died
    And dreamt he was alive,

Who thought he died and dreamt he saw
    A little nun in white
Come tip-toe in at twelve o'clock
    Bearing a candle-light.

The Juggler

I merely ordered buckwheat cakes
  With my most casual air,
Because it happened buckwheat cakes
  Were on the bill of fare
At four for twenty cents, and I
  Had twenty cents to spare.

I craved no notoriety;
  I thought till yesterday
That one might order buckwheat cakes
  With no whit more display
Than bacon, fish, spaghetti, ham,
  Plum cake, café au lait.

But I had failed to reckon with
  The joyous heart of man
That, even whelmed in kitchen smoke,
  Contributes what it can
To life's bright pageant of delight
  With flour and a frying pan.

A fellow lights a window up
  Where hundreds hurry by;
He pours a little disc of white
  Over a flame to fry:
He juggles a dawning buckwheat cake
  And flings it at the sky.

The Juggler

One side of it is creamy white,
  One side of it is brown;
And it twists and poises in mid-air
  Like a lithe circus clown;
And falls precisely—brown side up,
  And creamy-white side down!

This fellow bows not to the crowd
  Whose eyes are on him glued.
Through barriers of shiny glass
  He feeds the multitude
That hungers after beauty more
  Than it hungers after food.

And I, an all-but-pauper, sit
  Proud as a millionaire;
For I finance this festival
  With twenty cents to spare—
I merely order buckwheat cakes
  Upon the bill of fare.

On the Hill-Road

She lived alone; to all but three
    She never spoke a word:
God, Tabitha — her fluffy cat,
    And Dick, her singing bird.

Upon her dismal cottage door
    No neighbor ever knocked.
She kept the curtains safely drawn,
    She kept the windows locked.

Whene'er she ventured into town
    The gossips used to smile:—
She wore a little summer hat
    Ten summers out of style,

And triple skirts and frock and frills
    Of seasons long ago.
She wore a secret in her eye
    That men will never know.

Adventuresome, aloof, alone,
    What bitter thoughts will goad
A woman out of love and life
    And up an old hill-road?

Some talk romance and blighted vows;
    Some say she lost her mind.
Some meanly hinted sin and shame
    But none will ever find.

For secrets kept are secrets true
    When only three have heard:
God, Tabitha—her fluffy cat,
    And Dick, her singing bird.

Whitecaps

Many a sailor's drowned out there,
    Many a young girl wonders where.

The waves rise and the wind blows on them
    And reverently puts a white rose on them.

So much for love and poetry!
    The rhyming man should let the sea

Alone, and never turn his art
    To breaking of a woman's heart:

Telling her how the whitecaps are
    Little tombstones stretching far

Out on the graveyard of the deep,
    And one to mark her lover's sleep.

Dishonor to the rhyming man,
    Conceiving such a cruel plan—

Leaving a woman by the wave
    Forever guessing at a grave.

To a Pessimist

I will not walk nor talk with you
 Nor comfort your despair.
It not at all impresses me
 The way you tear your hair.

For I suspect all utter gloom
 As I suspect at night
The chapel walls wherein there burns
 No sanctuary light.

Obsequies

Finnerty's immortal soul
 May God save.
(How much do we pay the man
 Who dug his grave?)

In crown, glory and reward
 Be he a sharer.
(Did you bring mourning gloves
 For each pallbearer?)

Be kind to him, Lord of light,
 Mercy and hope,
(Now easy and down with him, men,
 And let go the rope!)

Peace may his spirit find
 With the eternal Lover.
(Now what are we going to do
 With the sods left over?)

Theories (*For Thomas Butler*)

"It may have many meanings,"
    My mother sweetly said,
As we sat and watched a night-star
    Falling overhead.

And then in her delightful way
    She told again the story
About the happy soul at last
    Released from Purgatory.

But this did not quite satisfy
    Barbara, John and me,
And we kept puzzling other things
    A falling star might be.

Perhaps it was a burning dart
    Of Michael or Gabriel,
And shot to scare the Evil One
    And keep him down in Hell.

Perhaps it was a little kiss
    The Holy Child was throwing,
Or maybe Our Lady's thimble dropped
    Today when she was sewing.

And while we grew more fanciful
    Up spoke Elizabeth:
"I bet old Uncle Christopher,
    Who smoked himself to death,

Was trying to steal another puff
    Up where the angels are,
And they just made him throw away
    The stub of his cigar!"

Song of the Meadow Boy

My father went driving a mowing-machine in
    the meadow,
My mother was running a sewing-machine in
    her room;
'Twas my father who fed us, winning our
    bread in the meadow,
While my mother was spinning our clothes
    from the wheel and the loom.
My father went out of a day to sleep in the
    meadow,
And many a sod did we lay to cover him all;
My mother kept shedding her strength in
    tears by the meadow—
Ah, snowy and white was the length of her
    funeral pall!

There is many a robin is preening his wings in
    the meadow,
For courting his love what fanciful things will
    he find!
They will wed and sing and drop and die in
    the meadow
And their nest will emptily swing and fall in
    the wind.

There are sounds full lonely tonight by the firs
    in the meadow,
And I mark when the cricket whirrs in the
    brake and the broom,
I am thinking I'm hearing a mowing-machine
    in the meadow,
Or is it a sewing-machine in a dark little room?

To My Grandfather

They tumble down in yonder lew,
    The little tomb-flowers over you:
The star-shroud wound around your grave
    Will flicker, for the cold winds wave.

But sleep. No wind will stir your dream;
    Gray dreamer, sleep by star and stream.
Your soul will find its warmth to-night
    At God's unbosomed firelight.

As white is white—O color of wings—
    Glow whitely where an old man sings!
Ye sparks of dawn in misted eyes,
    Relight in happy Paradise!

With all the aged Seraphim,
    Simeon, John and Joachim,
I wish you many an angel's song
    Where Heaven's afternoons are long.

Moonrise on Swampscott Beach

Without a splash or hiss the sun
    Sank in the bay.
The ocean swallowed all the light
    At the close of day.
The fishmen tied their little boats
    And hied away.

But I who lingered late and saw
    The darkness double,
Was much rewarded by the moon
    For all my trouble.
The drowning day sent up at last
    A silver bubble!

Ruins

The house we used to live in
    Was a sorry house and sad:
A roof, six windows and a door
    Was all the house we had.
        A house to laugh and love in—
        To climb and be above in—
        To quarrel and forgive in:
        The house we used to live in.

The house we used to dwell in
    Is a little house no more;
The windows sagged, the roof collapsed,
    The wind blew down the door.
        And never a light is found in—
        The spider makes no sound in—
        The cricket flutes his knell in
        The house we used to dwell in.

The house we all were born in!
    The day we left the town
I like to think it mourned for us
    So hard it tumbled down.
        And when the moonbeams stream in
        The house we used to dream in,
        No ghosts but ours will mourn in—
        And flit about forlorn in
        The house we all were born in.

Simplicity
(*For Francis Carlin*)

Now 'tis easy to rise
With the sun in the skies.
'Tis no labor to go
To the village below
With the people who pass
On the highroad to Mass,
And a young thrush adorning
With song the whole morning.

For devotion one needs
But a small pair of beads.
One has only to stand
When the book changes hand,
Or kneel in your pew
When the rest of them do.
And it's easy to tell
From three rings of the bell
When God is to come
To your breast for a home.

Now in weather like this
'Tis comparative bliss
And delight to be turning
To plowing and churning,
Or reaping the yield
Of the crops in the field.
A little brown egg
Is easy to beg

Simplicity

From under the breast
Of herself in the nest.
There is fleece in the fold
To protect you from cold
And a little gray mare
Carries one anywhere.

When the dark shadows fall
There is starlight for all.
Any stupid gossoon
Sees the man in the moon.
Any gentleman knows
If he brushes his clothes
And plucks a bouquet
From the bush on the way
And whistles a song
As he journeys along,

That some maiden or other
Will beg of her mother
Permission to wait
By the old cottage gate.
And it's often a meeting
Or simple love greeting
And a little tear shedding
Will end in a wedding.

One would never be missing
The time it takes kissing
Your old mother's brow
When the night has gone low.
A little white candle

Is easy to handle.
A short little prayer
At the head of the stair
Is easy to say
At the end of the day.
A few flowers and a stream
Are enough for a dream!

Sure the height of felicity
Lies in simplicity!

Transformation

The features may be beautiful or not
    On which we find it—
A smile takes half its beauty from the thought
    That lies behind it.

So when by her apple-cart old Nelly dozes
    On a wooden stool,
And dreams of golden lilies and sunlit roses
    In a silver pool,

At times a subtle loveliness and grace
    Will beautify
Her quivering mouth, her finely wrinkled face,
    And rheumy eye.

The Poet
(For Aunt Kate)

They say he's writing poems
About the sky and sea—
And putting flowers and angels
Where they never ought to be.

They say he scribbles verses
And tries to make you cry:
And every other word he writes
Is "star" or "butterfly".

They say he talks about the moon;
(And that is very bad)
And I hear he had a vision,
Or he makes believe he had.

I rub my eyes with wonderment,
It seems so like a dream.
Is this the boy who used to like
My tapioca cream?

For Padraic Pearse

Though for his wake there never burnt a candle
    Yet coffinless beneath a wall of shame,
An Irish lad loves death, as he loves beauty;
    There is a ring of freedom in the name.

For God's house is higher than a prison
    And surely keeps some starry window there,
Where martyred eyes may see poor Ireland weeping
    And tell how she is sad—but very fair.

O memories all beautiful with linnets
    Calling their love beneath the listening trees,—
While merry pipers trooping in to market
    Are fluting out your war-songs to the breeze!

O happy, happy dust that has no graveyard,
    That keening winds lift reverently above
And scatter by each pretty stile and meadow,
    A wedding with each sunny field you love!

The prayers of Irish motherhood at nightfall—
    What hero's death such epitaph could bring!
The love of little children down in Connacht
    Is better than the glory of a king.

The Guardian Angel

Seraph beside me, great Intelligence,
  Soft is thy footfall or I should hear;
And softer thy sigh in this deep night silence,
  When my own breathing thunders in my ear.

I lit me a candle and searched about me;
  I reached in the darkness but found no wings.
Is it I have been disillusioned
  In this, alas, as in other things?

Seraph whose breath runs white with music,
  Wilt thou no happy song repeat!
Art not ashamed when even the cricket
  Sings in my threshold so loud and sweet?

The Gifford Girl

Two dresses laid she by at night
    And loosed her flowing hair,
She rose at dawn and stood in fright
    And wondered which to wear.
Should it be white for her delight,
    Or black for her despair?

She saw a widow weep—and now
    She saw a laughing bride.
A little bit she laughed, but how
    More bitterly she cried!
And the wedding-veil upon her brow
    She very tightly tied.

She walked triumphantly at dawn
    Across the lonesome vale.
Beyond the dim boreen and lawn
    She heard a curlew wail.
She stood and tapped her fingers on
    The door of Richmond jail.

That Richmond jail might open wide
    She smote it with her hand.
"Who knocks?" the sleepy warden cried
    And could not understand.
A trembling, girlish voice replied:
    "A woman of Ireland!"

A hush that chilled the very stone
    Upon the prison fell.

* Grace Gifford, who married Joseph Mary Plunkett, poet and soldier, at
Richmond Barracks in Ireland, just before he was shot.

The Gifford Girl

Young Plunkett straightened up alone
    Within his narrow cell;
He bade the prison gong intone
    And be their wedding bell.

O ye who know a lover's grief
    And feel a lover's pride:
What gave this breaking heart relief
    And cheered this drooping bride?
What said this lover in the brief
    Last hour before he died?

Whatever lovers say—he said,
    And then he passed along.
They put a hood upon his head
    And bound it with a thong.
Then—England lost a ball of lead
    And Ireland lost a song.

A hero and a soldier, too,
    They buried him in lime.
Upon his wedding-morn they slew
    A lover in his prime.
Into a burning ditch they threw
    A poet and his rhyme.

O brood of riflemen, who vie
    With brute and knave and churl!
On Judgment Day I prophesy
    You'll hear his ashes swirl—
And God will make you stare it, eye
    For eye, with the Gifford girl.

A Fledgeling Robin

Take us size for size and he
    Is but a speck aside of me.
His gold-rimmed lip
    Is but my finger tip;
His tiny throat—
    A button on my coat!

Or take us age for age and I
    Am older immeasurably
By twenty years or so.
    Three weeks ago
He was a wee, blue egg at rest
    Under his mother's breast.

Or take us soul for soul; he knows
    None of life's bitter, bitter woes,
No endless tears,
    No agonizing fears,
No hopes of immortality
    That ever try and trouble me.

Yet turn us both into a wood some May,
    Some fresh, fair morn and listen all the day
How very deftly he
    Creates more poetry
With three soft-gurgled notes, than I attain
    By a whole life of pain!

In the Everlasting City

Vestiges

Oh, who can mark how swift it all is done,
 Or reckon up or gauge—can anyone?—
These vestiges of beauty in the grass,
 Where mites and moles and shimmering
  sunbeams pass!

How much omnipotence past our divining
 Is there required to keep the firefly shining,
The moth breathing or the dark snail crawling,
 Or the little, tree-top whip-poor-will from
  falling!

And does life's Lord allow to trouble Him
 The churning of colors on a bubble brim—
A robin-hop—a twinkling of a wing—
 And is He charmed to hear a starling sing!

The fluttering and exquisitely frail,
 Wide rainbow-targets on the peacock's tail;
The shuddering humming-bird and
  wind-blown bee,
 Were these decreed and planned eternally!

There's much of mystery howe'er you look
 In the splash and gurgle of a running brook.
I've seen rare starlight shining in a well;
 I've heard strange murmurings in a
  small sea-shell.

Out of the chrysalis a butterfly;
 Out of the burnished seed a goldenrod:—
Waving a plume or petal to the sky,
 These foot-tracks of the journeyings of God.

The Painters

Would not quarrel with a star
 For being high and I so low;
And so I will not quarrel
 With Fra Angelico.
He fashioned our Virgin Lady fair
 And put what stars around her hair—
What flawless lilies on her dress,
 And in her eyes what tenderness—
Yet when could artist ever trace
 For any man his mother's face!

Rather I quarrel with the earth,
 Too dull and colorless below
To heighten the imagining
 Of even Fra Angelico.
For lilies never grow in Spring
 As white as Mary's mantling,
And all the shades of sunlight strewn
 On rainbow, field-flower and moon
Were never fitted to impress
 One fragment of her loveliness.

My brush has never made a mark;
 I have no canvases to show;—
And no Madonnas have I wrought
 To rival Fra Angelico.
Palette and pigments none I keep
 To trouble his immortal sleep.
My brow no laurel-wreaths beseem;
 Yet have I somehow had a dream
Of a white canvas that will lie
 Unfinished, Mother, till I die.

The Welcome

No music He heard, and no angels He saw
    As He lay in His wrappings of linen and straw;
And the ox and the ass could not kneel and adore
    For the poor creatures never were angels before.

The palace He found was an old cattle stall
    With a broken-down roof and a windowless wall,
And it looked so ashamed of its spider-worn wood;
    But it tried to be Heaven, as well as it could.

A dull stable-lantern that hung dark and dim
    Was the small bit of moonlight that flickered on Him.
Now it longed to be beautiful, starry and bright,
    And it sputtered and wept for the dearth of its light.

But a Lady of Beauty stood over His head
    While she gathered the strewings about for His bed.
And her soul was as sweet as a fresh-budding rose
    And as white as the fusion of myriad snows.

And her hands did not soil this immaculate prize,
    And her breath did not sully the bloom in His eyes.
On her breast sweet and safe could He slumber and nod:
    The lily-white village-maid, Mother of God.

Nails

Whenever the bright blue nails would drop
Down on the floor of his carpenter shop,
Saint Joseph, prince of carpenter men,
Would stoop to gather them up again;
For he feared for two little sandals sweet,
And very easy to pierce they were
As they pattered over the lumber there
And rode on two little sacred feet.

But alas, on a hill between earth and heaven
One day—two nails in a cross were driven,
And fastened it firm to the sacred feet
Where once rode two little sandals sweet;
And Christ and His mother looked off in death
Afar—to the valley of Nazareth,
Where the carpenter's shop was spread with dust
And the little blue nails, all packed in rust,
Slept in a box on the window-sill;
And Joseph lay sleeping under the hill.

A Gift of Flowers

A basket of roses for the Royal House of David—
  A harvest of blossoms in the Spring.
Chrysanthemums and daisies for the ladies of Jerusalem
  And lilies for the daughters of the King.

Lilies out in Galilee, opening in April—
  Sunflowers to pluck and carry home;
Poppies for high priestesses and myriads of tulips
  For the wives of the Emperors of Rome.

But ah, come and wander, meek Maid of Nazareth,
  Wander by the brook and by the lea;
A sweet, little, meek, frail, lonely-by-the wayside,
  Shadow-blue violet for thee!

A Field of Wheat

A Field of Wheat

'Tis midnight and the prairie owl is lazy by the lake,
And half of him is sleeping, for half of him is sly,
But one side of his ugly face is very wide awake
With the moonbeams of midnight in his eye.

'Tis starlight and the prairie owl is watching the tall sheaves,
Those tireless, ever-twisting, swishy silences of grain,
All tangled and wind-laced and fluttering their leaves
And murmuring and moaning in their pain.

"Some of us," they whisper, "shall ripen in the Spring
And feed the hungry multitudes beyond the land and sea,
And some of us shall tremble on the table of the King,
Ah, which of us, dear brothers, shall it be?"

"And which of us shall falter when the wagon load is high,
And fall from the heavy harvest when the men are
    hauling in,

A Field of Wheat

And trampled in the darkness of the furrows shall we lie
And dream forevermore what might have been!"

"O Sacred Bread, O mystic Host, O snowy Gown of God!
O dream of every blade of wheat that flickers in the
     sun—
And shall we rise up beautiful and fragrant from the sod
And be the raiment for the Holy One?"

'Tis starlight and the prairie owl has let his eyelid close,
For tired heads must droop at last and birds
     may slumber sweet;
But the waves rise, and the waves fall, and only the
     wild wind knows
The everlasting restlessness of wheat.

The Little Flower

Knowing that it would burn she courted fire;
  And who shall wish to chide her heart's desire?

For when the little altar-rose was sweet
  And withering beside the candle heat,
And when she saw a beautiful, white moth—
  Its wings drop flaming to the altar-cloth:

Long did she ponder would it not be right
  To brave the pain if she but reach the light
And be Love's fuel as a moth, a rose,
  And fall where all earth's bitter beauty goes.

For beauty runneth out as quick as sun,
  Quick as a nun lights candles, one by one
For Vespers; swift as swallow-shadows pass
  Or field mice trickle through the flowing grass.

Alas for all the violet petals shed
  And all last Summer's lilies that are dead!—
For hollyhocks, laburnum, marigold
  And whatsoever names the flowers hold!

She heard the bells above the convent chime;
  She dreamt of that eternal seeding-time
When starry soil and loam of azure field
  Would be her substance and her colors yield.

And so the flame became her heart's desire;
  Knowing that it would burn, she courted fire—
She who had seen upon the altar-cloth
  The rose's dust, the ashes of a moth!

Mater Pulcherrima

Did God this virgin mold,
Her hair a goldener gold,
Her eye a bluer blue,
Piercing, transfixing you
If haply you should meet
Her on the busy street?
Having of mother need,
Did God excel, exceed,
Within, without no less,
Bestowing loveliness?
Or how would she compare
With maids we reckon fair,
Whose look I forfeit now
With vigilance and vow?

"Peace, peace," my angel said,
Turning away his head,
"Be for a while content
With aching wonderment.
She waits a-top a stair;
Climb bruised and bleeding there.
Let folk declare you died
Restless, unsatisfied.
If by Christ's help you be
Ransomed eternally,
Then should her beauty, scanned,
Fall shy of what you planned—
Hush! Can you doubt a bit
God missed His mark a whit
When He was put to it?"

Saint Stanislaus

A brief light,
  A brief flower,
Upon a shrine
  A little hour.

He died young
  Yet he died
Pale and wan
  And hollow-eyed.

Too slim and slender
  To control
The fiery churnings
  Of his soul.

By heart-thunder
  And spirit-flash
Withered to cinder
  And burnt to ash.

A brief flower,
  A brief light
Upon an altar
  A single night.

All stem, all lily,
  And no soil.
All taper, all flame
  And no oil.

An Elegy for the Jesuit Graveyard at Woodstock

There is a graveyard that I know, with never a bird's
  sweet lay:
  Where never a mourning wreath is laid, and never
  a tear has flown;
Where children pass by a railed fence—but never a
  child to pray
  For the dead who lie dark-shrouded and alone.

Oh, manhood has gallantly gone, and reckoned
  not the pain;
  Quenched in an urn of dreamy death and
  damp fallow land:—
Old priests in their long stoles, white and straightly lain,
  And the withering splendor of a young priest's hand.
Green hills rise and valleys droop to hold a
  yellow stream,
  Ever anon, anon and ever, in the slow wash of the wind;
You say they sleep a worthless sleep and dream a
  worthless dream:
  Ah, weep not, traveller, but do not be unkind!

Up from these ashes goes a flame, a red mystic ghost,
  'Tis the sinner's secret, here burnt and never to be told.
Sometimes you fancy you might hear the
  sound of a breaking Host,
  Whenever the dead twigs crackle in the cold.

The woodland stirs with a Latin prayer; the
  trees in black are bound,

An Elegy

And bordered with a golden fringe, the leaves
   turn one by one.
The office of Virgin, Confessor, is sung in a windy sound
   And nature bids the breviary prayers go on.

Hillock of green and hillock of green, with
      coverlet stretching wide,
   Oh, what a garden this land would make if
      one were planted here:
For up from the priestly dust that drank the
      wine from Jesus' side
   Might not the reddest rose in the world appear!

A little shower of grave-stones stand along in a
      circled row,
   With many a shade of whiteness, and a name
      carved above;
Names no race will ever wear, no generation show—
   Names cancelled now in a mighty stroke of love.

Dark-lanterned mariner, who steer your ship of night,
   Where decks are strangely littered with the
      tread of ghostly feet,
Your prow turns golden in the moon; your sail
      a magic white—
   There is no death if death but be complete.

'Tis only half-way dying that makes life's chalice sad.
   This is the sermon told from stars to the dull
      sod beneath;
But they who have gone in nakedness, in
      wondrous light are clad,
   They taste and see how sweet are the depths of death.

An Elegy

Death to them was a little maid with deep and
   wondrous eyes,
  With dark hair and white lips, and an accent
   soft and mild;
Daughter of doom, and yet she sang of life, of Paradise—
  And lent to men the vision of a child.

Windows were for looking through to watch
   the Heavens fair:—
  Halls went curving chapelward, where saintly
   feet had trod.
Rooms were a battlefield for men to struggle
   at their prayer,
  And all things were a ladder unto God.

Music was a rift of joy re-echoing from Heaven,
  A lost shred of fair delight from Lady Mary's choir.
They rendered beauty unto Him from Whom
   it first was given,
  Now beauty is a thing beyond desire.

Dear God of lonely graveyards, take loveliness away:
  Take every bud and blossom, and radiant birds that sing!
Place them where the timid sleep, or the weak
   are laid for aye;
  These want no tears and need no sorrowing.

Angelicus*

Are we unseemly when we name him thus,
Too proud, importunate, presumptuous?
Is it a certain rash conceit in us
To dare to call a man "Angelicus"—
To plume a child of Adam with a name
That flaming Seraphs, Thrones and Powers claim;
To dignify the dust from which we spring
With such supreme unwonted blazoning?
I can imagine those who never fell,
The brothers tall of stately Gabriel,
Sunning themselves in all the light that falls
From God's face and hurls upon the walls
The would-be shadows of invisible things—
Huge undulating silhouettes of wings,
(Most strange existences, this shapeless host
Of sighing moths about the Holy Ghost,
Warmed by the beauteous, uncreated flame)—
I fancy them all smiling at the name,
Or charmed at our extreme naïveté,
Our almost-apotheosis of clay,
Saying we are too rash to name him thus,
Too proud, importunate, presumptuous,
Calling it rare and high conceit in us
To dare to call a man "Angelicus."

Angel of God, who sing in Heaven's tower,
High handiwork of our Creator's power,
Unfettered intellect and sun-lit will,
Glittering upon each steeple-top and hill

*For the feast of Saint Thomas Aquinas.

Angelicus

Of Heaven's holy city; it is true
How all contemptible aside of you
Is man and man's condition which I own
Meekest, most unlovely, last and lone
Of all His creatures which the Lord inspires
With quenchless dreams and desperate desires.
Man is a reckless, none too certain scheme,
Spirit and dust confounded in a dream,
The borderland of reason, freedom's term,
The twilight of an angel and a worm.
One lower ladder-rung and gone would be
His last few threads of rationality.
The painful offspring of a man and maid
Who once walked in a garden unafraid;

Branded, disgraced and stumbling in his sins,
A mite of ashes in a world that spins,
A little wind-blown spark from out a fire,
A low untunable string upon a lyre.
A wavering candle mimicking a star,
Confounding nothingness with things that are,
Kinsman to cattle, reasonable fool,
A lily's image in a muddy pool,
A twinkling ember vaguely now discerned
When the grate is cooling and the logs are burned.
Yet, angel of God, unrivaled in your bliss,
Suppose you had been such a one as this!
Suppose that spirit-principle in you
Enkindling will and holding reason true,
The fundament of all your life, the flame
That robes you with existence and a name—

Angelicus

Suppose it had been burdened, ballasted
With the flesh's heaviness, the body's lead;
And all day long you had a hill to climb
And crawled your passage one step at a time,
The eagle in you yearning to be free,
But bondsman to the law of gravity!

Suppose that spirit-torch you hold so proud
Were faltering, blown at, hidden in a shroud!
Suppose you had some other thing to do
Besides to think and love; and over you
The meaningless dumb stars blinked in the sky
And challenged you to find the reason why!
Let us suppose, O bright Angelic one,
That you were Thomas, Count Aquino's son.
You came into this world, began to be
On a little farm in southern Italy,
Helpless as any whelp a lion lays
Upon some straw along the mountain ways.
With God your aim, Infinity your goal.
You lay a barren and bewildered soul
And learned by tiresome processes aright
The simplest messages of sound and sight—
Fumbling in wonderment with hands and eyes,
Staring for months in stupor at the skies.
Suppose this process were a thing of years,
Clouded with laughter, doubt and sudden fears,
A journey of abstractions you must plod
From sound and color to the realm of God;
And when some filtered loveliness seeped through
And Truth seemed sweetly beckoning to you,

Angelicus

The mill-wheel of your breath would cease to rush,
Fatigue would raise its hand and whisper "Hush"—
The brooklets of your blood would slacken down
Like lights and noises fading in a town
And drowsiness and sleep would mark you there
The helpless prey to respite and repair.

Angel of God—calmly and palely white,
With all this cloud between him and the light,
With all this heavy harness round him hurled,
Lo, Count Aquino's son looked at the world!
His eyes were lit with wonder and with youth,
He saw Romance and knew her name was Truth.
Beyond all grace of maiden was she fair;
He longed to pluck one rosebud for her hair.
They say his laughter ran like water sweet,
His countenance was fresh as ripening wheat;
His was the trysting place where God would stroll,
The moonlight and the gardens of the soul.
And like to one, who, from a sea-girt wall,
In diving, cleaves the multicolored fall
Of purple waters, where the ocean swirls,
In quest of deep and unremembered pearls;
He stripped himself and plunged into the tide
Wherein this hinted beauty might abide.
He sought a meaning for the things that be
And spanned the orbit to Infinity.
He delved where truth all sunk and hidden lay
And from its roots he pulled the weeds away
Into the tunnels of God's hidden plan
The silver floodlights of his genius ran.

Angelicus

He pieced together every secret thing
That had its birth in human reasoning:
Creation's purposes; effect and cause;
Virtues and acts, and essence and its laws;
The rules of thought, the canons of the mind;
Cosmos and chaos; spirits and their kind;
The Holy Ghost, the Father and the Son,
The triune splendor of the Three in One;
Sin and rebellion and the Primal Fall;
God's Virgin Mother and the Angels all;
The will, emotions, instinct and desire;
Rulers and governments and freedom's fire;
Justice and rights and what a king must give,
And what must be a slave's prerogative;
God's gifts of grace; His wondrous Incarnation;
Redemption, immortality, salvation,—
From Heaven's heights his sweeping vision fell
Down to the nethermost dark cave of hell;
Each revelation, gospel, mystery
He channelled, blended into harmony—
Truth chimed with truth, and when his work was done
They swung like ordered planets round the sun.

And then, while life and manhood still were young,
His treatises declared, his poems sung,
Poor Thomas of Aquino felt the tip
Of death's cold finger resting on his lip;
Those limpid concepts in his minds full store
Mixed, grew strangely cloudy, and were no more.

Angelicus

Alas, mayhap may never be again
Such matchless wedding of a soul and brain.
Of countless pities, this a pity I
Do reckon, much beyond all tear and sigh:
That Seraphim may sing, but men must die!

Angel of God, we seek a name to crown
This hero's high achievement and renown.
We've reached beyond the borders of the blue
And borrowed him an epithet from you.
But—if it be too rash to name him thus,
Unseemly, arrogant, presumptuous—
Denoting something of conceit in us
To title such a one "Angelicus"—
With none the less of triumph in our boast
We'll count all titles worthless at the most,
And bowing low to God's creative plan
We'll call the Angel of the Schools— a man.

At the Consecration

I thought the rising sun upon
   The rim of sky and sea
Would be the morning's fairest gift
   Of vision unto me.

Until I caught a glimpse of God
   When He was raised in air
Above the white horizon
   Of an old priest's hair.

The Way of the Cross

Along the dark aisles
   Of a chapel dim,
The little lame girl
   Drags her withered limb.

And all alone she searches
   The shadows on the walls
To find the three pictures
   Where Jesus falls.

The Holy One of Mary

And this is He whom Heaven hymns,
All trembling in His white young limbs,
Whom choirs adore and seraphs bless—
Unspeakable His helplessness.
A Baby's cheek the wind would kindle.
Ah, holy weaver and blessed spindle,
That spun the little swaddling clothes
To sheathe so sweet, so fair a rose!
Dull stable-lamp, my love you are—
Shine bright and be His morning star.
Full many a moon would give her light
To hang upon your beam to-night,
And flood the wondrous sanctuary
And shine on Him and His Mother Mary.

O Sacred Love and Life and Law
Whose mercy-mingled power I draw
To live, to breathe, and be aware
Of sunlight and the brimming air!
Great Bosom whence my spirit sprang;
For Whom my soul in hunger sang;
O white with Age that overflows
The showering of a million snows;
Sinew and Strength and Might unriven,
Upholder of the stars and Heaven,
How camest Thou to choose a stall?

The Holy One of Mary

Ah, Little Brother, how small, how small!
What need to know the bitter cold
Eternal One—an hour old!
And yet did not the Eternal Three
Foreknow how bitter the cold would be!

The dark comes over this little town,
A woman is pulling her shutter down;
A woman is making her window bright,
To welcome her Saviour on Christmas night.
The clouds are draping the starless hill,
The moon is quenched at the Father's will,
The Angels are crowding the snowy moor,
A lantern hangs on the chapel door,
The sounds of the singers arise and pass;
A beggar is crawling to Midnight Mass.
The shadowy winds are still awhile
The children turn in their sleep and smile.
May God have mercy and shield us well
Who hear the stroke of the midnight bell!

"Good-night, sweet Jesu, and take Thy rest,
Be happy now in Thy narrow nest,
Thou must not notice Thy mother weep—
Hear her lullaby and go to sleep!"

The Lonely Crib

I pity the slender Mother-maid
    For the night was dark and her heart afraid
As she knelt in the straw where the beasts had trod
    And crooned and cooed to the living God.

And I pity Saint Joseph whose heart wept o'er
    The ruined stall and the broken floor
And the roof unmended for Him and her,—
    And to think himself was a carpenter!

O Thrones, Dominions, spirits of power,
    Where were you there in that bitter hour!
And where the Cherubim-wings withal
    To cover the wind-holes in the wall!

Three lambs a shepherd-boy brought, and these
    Were Powers and Principalities;
And Ariel, Uriel, angels bright,
    Were two frail rays from a lantern-light.

The faded eyes of a wondering ass
    Were dreamy mirrors where visions pass.
And a poor old ox in the stable dim,
    His moo was the song of the Seraphim!

Father Hopkins' Mystic Songs

The Holy Ghost, who is a dove,
    Building a nest
    Within his breast,
Feathered his soul with downy love.

Softly, little winds of grace,
    To tall-in-the-breeze,
    Eternal trees
Would he arise in your embrace.

The trail of echoes he had heard
    His heart would follow
    As a swift swallow
Where distance glorifies a bird.

His eyes had need of some far vision;
    His note was stayed
    Whose throat was made
To melody in lanes Elysian.

Oh may not one with mouth and wings
    Who was too weak
    His cage to break
Be pardoned if he strangely sings!

A Priest's Offertory

Had I a whiter host to give
In snowier garments wouldst Thou live.
Thine were a chalice rich and old
Had I a better thing than gold.
Thy wine-press would know the sweet
Warm treading of an angel's feet.
Thy wheatfields were grown afar
In the soft meadow-land of star.
If priceless linen could I buy
Upon such linen wouldst Thou lie;
Something more virginal than bees
Would spin Thee purer lights than these.
I'd, going, borrowing, take a hymn
From the white, born-singing Seraphim.
I'd plunder beauty in the night,
Star-stripping yonder worlds of light,
I'd color-strip each wondrous, rare
High-blooming, low-blooming, radiant there
Refolded flower, firm and fair
In a green-valleyed everywhere.
(Christ's Mother! Attend this feast.
Gift-load to-day His giftless priest.)

A Priest's Offertory

Midnight one night was still,
Heaven was whitening a hill;
Dark floundered in the wave of morn,
Infinite Infancy was born.
Eternal Power sank below,
A frail white miracle of snow.
Eternal Wonder left the skies
And dwindled into two soft eyes,
Child limbs that could not reach,
Child lips that knew no speech
Spoken,—save the murmurings heard
From breathing beast, wind and bird.
The unbeginning God began
To live the long slow hours of man.
His Mother, bending her fair head,
Straw-gathering—she laid His bed.
A whirling star-world came and halted
Above a blown-roofed, low, thatch-vaulted
Cave— Ah! are we not agreed
'Twas piteous royalty indeed!

And yet beyond an Infant's sleep
Found He a hiddenness more deep.
Finds it each morning when I stand,
He, in the curved holding of my hand.
Starlight is light but ill,
Star-shadow—darker still:
The lone firefly that wields
His fine blue lantern in the fields
Is far more luminous than Thou
Who hideth Thine endless splendor—how!

The rose more glory has to rate her
Lovelier than the Rose-Creator.
The violet is mantled finer
Than the world's own Flower-Designer,
Hill-Builder and Meadow-Weaver,
Earth-Waker, Cloud-Conceiver.
The blind beggar, kneeling while I pass
Through the sweet words old, told in the Mass,
Sunnier visions light his dreams
Than Thine, dark-locked—in death, it seems.
Covered indeed—and covered how!
Veil-shielded lest perchance I know
Not when the long day is sped:
Ah! is this Jesus or is it bread?
I, Christ, who brought Thee down,
Must label Thee, to know mine own,
Must light a swinging lamp on high,
Lest all men, turning, pass Thee by.
Thou knowest my voice upon the wine;
Faith knoweth Thee—but no eyes of mine.

Wings fell, swords fell, scabbards fell
Into the yawning throat of Hell;
An Angel host—O Heaven's loss!—
Would not adore Thee on the Cross.
Yet on the Cross when Thou wert lain
Could they not see what love was slain?
Observed they not Thy Godly mien,
How Thou didst welcome death, serene?
How deeper, broader Hell would be
If Lucifer were asked to see
And worship as we worship Thee.

A Priest's Offertory

(Ah, when I speak the words that bring
Such helplessness on Heaven's King
Well, little Mass-bell, mightest thou ring.)
Rise manhood, in me rise!
Desire, aspire to sacrifice.
See how His warm blood stains the cup,
Now with Himself lift thyself up.
His paten is a burst of gold,
How much of offering will it hold?
Will it hold youth,—its bloom and glow?
(These wilt Thou garner anyhow.)
Will He take friend and loved one still?
(The weed-strewn graveyard cries— "He will.")
By Thee made, fashioned, let live,
What may I free, untrammeled give?

I give Thee a poor man bearing his load
Along the poor man's bleak highroad;
Now scorned—now pointed at with glee;
"Yon fool wears Christ's mean livery!"

I give Thee an angel?—somewhat less,
Yet wishing an angel's stainlessness,
Hoping Thy sunny love may yield
A lily in a trampled field.
I give Thee unchallenged, full control,
Of what is empire in my soul.
I lead Thee up the palace stair
Of mine own heart—enthrone Thee there!
If but a king forsooth may sing
And be content to be a king;
Unto Thee now, my vows renewed,
I stamp and seal my servitude.
I here proclaim Thy courts are fair;
Charmeth and pleaseth me the air.
I love the whole-souled, full-rolled ring
Of war and front-line soldiering,
Of men who bled—and when they fell—
Did judge the tribes of Israel.

Strip me of buckler, sword and lance,
But Captain—let us both advance!
Keep my poor eyes firm-fixed upon
The altar where God slays His Son.
O Father, Son and Holy Ghost,
I would I had a whiter host!